Derek's Words

Speaking Without Words

Diana Gutoskie
APRIL, 2017.

Diana Gutoskie

DEREK'S WORDS
Copyright © 2016 by Diana Gutoskie

All rights reserved. Neither this publication nor any part of this publication may be reproduced or transmitted in any form or by any means, electronic or mechanical, including photocopying, recording or any information storage and retrieval system, without permission in writing from the author.

All Scripture quotations taken from Common English Bible (CEB). All rights reserved. No part of these materials may be reproduced or transmitted in any form or by any means, electronic or mechanical, including photocopying and recording, or by any information storage or retrieval system, except as may be expressly permitted by the 1976 Copyright Act, the 1998 Digital Millennium Copyright Act, or in writing from the publisher.

Printed in Canada

ISBN: 978-1-4866-1346-5

Word Alive Press
131 Cordite Road, Winnipeg, MB R3W 1S1
www.wordalivepress.ca

Library and Archives Canada Cataloguing in Publication

Gutoskie, Diana, 1954-, author
    Derek's words / Diana Gutoskie.
Issued in print and electronic formats.
ISBN   978-1-4866-1346-5   (paperback).--ISBN   978-1-4866-1347-2 (ebook)

    1. Grief. 2. Loss (Psychology). 3. Grandchildren--Death--Psychological aspects. I. Title.

| BF575.G7G88 2016 | 155.9'37 | C2016-903218-3 |
| | | C2016-903219-1 |

In memory of Derek Chase Gutoskie
April 20, 1998 to February 20, 2005.

Jesus said to his disciples, "*Whoever welcomes this child in my name welcomes me. Whoever welcomes me, welcomes the one who sent me. Whoever is least among you all is the greatest*" (Luke 9:48).

This book is for others whose hearts have been broken by the loss of a little one. But it's also for me, Derek's grandma, to capture my love and connection with my grandson.

Derek, Lindsay, with their mom, Michele

Foreword

Telling my story is not easy. For a long time, I put off writing even though some said it would be cleansing and healing.

This is a story about love and hope. It's a story of my struggle to preserve the blessings of my grandson Derek's life against the hopelessness of his disability and death. My hope is that these words will somehow make a difference in your life, especially if your own heart has been broken.

Who am I to tell you this story? I'm Derek's grandmother. Watching him live and die in my arms gives me the right to tell you my story. I know firsthand the deep sadness and helplessness, and even frustration, anger and resentment that come from watching a beloved child suffer.

I am a reader, not a writer—in fact I don't even like to write. Where reading entertains and calms me, writing causes me stress and anxiety. I am a restless, intense person, sometimes talkative sometimes not. I like people, nature, dogs and books, sometimes (actually most of the time) not in that order.

I am a Christian and believer in God—not a biblical scholar. I can't quote you Bible verse after Bible verse. My faith walk is inconsistent and flounders often. But I know what I know. I do get peace and hope from Bible readings and I have added some of the many passages that have been meaningful to me in hopes that they will be a comfort to you.

My understanding is that everyone's life contains love and loss. I am learning that what defines me is not the loss so much as how I respond to that loss. To lose a grandson has taught me how helpless I really am. It is not the natural order of life for a grandparent to bury their grandchild. It has stripped me of any illusions of control I might have thought I had.

I have learned the *why* questions of life are pointless. Faced with Derek's death, I have found I know even less than ever before. However, this is what I do know: God doesn't fix things for me. There was no fairness in Derek's disability or his painful death. Derek was born with a disability that was no one's fault.

But I have also learned the truth that God is present with me. He promises:

> *When you pass through the waters, I will be with you; when through the rivers, they won't sweep over you. When you walk through the fire, you won't be scorched and flame won't burn you.* (Isaiah 43:2)

Derek's Words

This is my story—mine and Derek's. It's not an easy story but I hope it will help you find peace and healing as you walk through your life after the loss of a loved one. There is no going around or over grief—the walk is through the fire of loss

Derek and Lindsay

Derek hanging out at the pool

1

What's wrong with Derek? This was the question asked by his parents and loved ones at his birth on April 20, 1998. *He looks perfect—how can anything be wrong?*

Of course it wasn't so simple. The answer to what was wrong was long and detailed.

Derek was born with a genetic disorder. There were many other things wrong with Derek: he had a total disability. That meant his brain did not tell the rest of his body what to do. After the age of nine months, he was not able to eat so he used a feeding tube, and was thus categorized as technology dependent.

Did Derek have intellectual ability? The experts would say no, but I believe he did only it was trapped inside his body.

Anyone who saw him knew the obvious: he couldn't walk; his arms and legs flailed out of control. He couldn't use words, although he communicated with emotion and energy. Many people couldn't understand him but those who loved and cared for him understood him perfectly.

Derek could feel the mood in his environment and would respond to it. When he felt fear, he would pout his little lip and cry. He showed real, pure joy and would laugh straight from his belly. Most of the time Derek's responses were extreme: he cried hard and laughed equally as hard.

Derek fought hard to survive. He didn't have what the world views as important— such as a high I.Q.—but he had the hidden values that the world longs to find. Derek had contentment, happiness and love. When Derek was with the people who loved and cared for him, his face was full of smiles. He had what he wanted: love and someone to hold him close. He had what the world is searching for.

Sometimes when someone is having a baby we say things like, "I just want him/her to be healthy." What happens when this isn't the case?

What does the Bible teach us about the value of all people?

Have you ever known someone like Derek who might seem like they don't have what's important—but they actually possess what's most important? What did you learn from knowing them? How did it change you?

2

It was February 2005. Derek was living with his dad—my son Kevin—his mom, Michele, and his sister, Lindsay, in Plattsville, Ontario. He was almost seven years old.

I had begun to fulfill a lifelong dream of working in another province. Having witnessed firsthand Derek's fighting spirit to live life to the fullest, I took the leap in my own life to accept a job opportunity as a mental health therapist in Revelstoke, British Columbia. I loved my time, working with the people, and living nestled in the mountains. My husband Danny was in Ontario. Our habit was to talk daily by phone. When I talked to Danny on Sunday, February 13, he was worried because Derek was "really sick". This did not concern me as Derek over the years had been really sick many times. "Really sick" had become the family phrase for when Derek had trouble breathing and needed oxygen. He would get congested, be unable to sleep and usually needed to be held most of the time.

I talked with Michele the next evening. Yes, Derek was "really sick". Somehow it was at that moment that I sensed this time was different. Michele didn't say so but I knew.

The next day, Tuesday, I went to work. My job was extremely busy and intense and it was easy for me to lose myself in my work. That evening I called Michele again. Derek was still "really sick".

I didn't sleep well that night—and I am usually a very good sleeper. Wednesday I again went to work, but I felt restless and anxious. I couldn't concentrate, and I *knew* my fear was coming true: Derek was dying. I cannot answer how I knew; it was just in my heart, although I could not accept it in my mind.

I went home for lunch but I couldn't eat. I phoned Danny and left him a message that I was going to get a flight to Toronto as soon as possible. I went back to work, asked my secretary, Cathy, to cancel my appointments for the rest of the day and week, as I needed to fly home because my grandson was ill.

Cathy, bless her kind heart, didn't ask any more questions. I had the sense, however, that she thought I was acting very weird. And I was, in fact, acting weird. I felt like I was in shock.

I booked a flight online from Kelowna to Toronto, for Thursday morning, the soonest flight available. Then I left a message with my supervisor that I needed to fly home to Ontario due to a family emergency. I left work as I could not concentrate.

At home, I put on my pajamas and started cleaning my house. Normally I hate house cleaning but I clean when I need to make changes or do something that I don't want to do. My co-worker, Paulette, who is a great person and friend, stopped in after work to see how I was doing. I told her I needed to go home to help my little Derek die. The stark truth of that statement made me physically ill. If I had had a choice about it, this was something I truly didn't want to do, but I knew Derek needed me. So did my family.

That statement was also my acknowledgement that the miracle I wanted from God—that God would show my family that he was real and really God by healing Derek completely—was not going to happen. I now know that my belief had nothing to do with God letting me or Derek down. This belief was about the myth that if only I had enough faith anything in my life would be fixed.

The Bible says, "*Faith is the reality of what we hope for, the proof of what we don't see*" (Hebrews 11:1). This is a description of what faith *does* more than what it *is*. If you continue to read the book of Hebrews, you will read about many men and women whose faith did not get the healing or fixes they wanted, yet they were blessed by God. In other words, their faith did not fix anything in this world.

I know now that Derek's death had nothing to do with me not having enough faith but at the time I wasn't sure.

When I think of faith now, I think of the well-known verse that says, "*God so loved the world that he gave his only Son, so that everyone who believes in him won't perish but will have eternal life*" (John 3:16). Thus, faith is about eternal life, for me and Derek and for all of us.

Have you ever had the experience of just knowing that something was going to happen? How do you understand this experience? Do you see it as a gift from God?

It's very hard when we have to do something we don't want to do. When you think of doing something that is extremely difficult emotionally, what motivates you?

How have you responded when God has not answered your desperate prayers for a miracle? Do you believe that "if only I had enough faith anything in my life would be fixed"? Is this biblical or not? How do you define faith?

3

That night I slept well, got up early, drove the four hours to Kelowna, flew to Toronto, rented a car and drove to Plattsville. The drive from Toronto was treacherous due to a snowstorm, but I was on a mission.

I arrived at my son Kevin's house around 10 p.m.

This may seem strange. I had never seen a person die. I do not have a medical background so I didn't know the physical signs that show that death is coming. The nurses who cared for Derek daily did not see the signs of death. Here's the strange part: as soon as I saw Derek, I knew that he was leaving us.

Before my arrival, Derek had been very agitated although his mom was holding him. I touched Derek's head and rubbed his legs, which he loved me to do. He calmed down and Michele was able to put him in his bed to sleep for a couple of hours.

The next day, Friday, Derek's nurse came to care for him. She thought Derek was feeling better as he was calmer. Derek's sister, Lindsay's birthday had been that week (February 16) but her party was going to be that night. Kevin was coming home early from work to fix her favourite meal, his homemade hamburgers. I went to the grocery store to pick up a birthday cake and some balloons for the party. I also went shopping and bought myself a suit to wear for Derek's funeral although I didn't say this to anyone, not even myself.

After school, Lindsay's friends came over. Kevin barbecued the hamburgers. Derek's nurse stayed late into the evening. Derek was enjoying the party and was either calm or sleeping. The nurse kept saying he was getting better. I sensed he was holding on for Lindsay's party.

After the meal, we—Kevin, Michele, Lindsay, her friends and I—went snow tubing. It felt so good. We didn't take Derek because he wasn't well but in the past when we took him on the toboggan, he loved the wind and would laugh and laugh.

My husband, Danny, arrived. He kept saying to me, "Derek is not good, is he?" All I could do was nod. I could not verbalize any words.

The next morning, I got up early to care for Derek so that Kevin and Michele could get some rest after a long night of being up with their son. I loved to rock and hold Derek. Oh, how I savoured that day with him. I kept telling him it was going to be okay.

Later that morning Michele called Derek's doctor and told her how ill he was. Derek was scheduled to go to the Child and Parent Resource Institute the next day, Sunday. Since he had daily nursing care at home, his doctor told Michele she would see Derek on Sunday.

My youngest son, Jason, and his wife, Charlene, who live up the street from Kevin were going to look at a new vehicle. Kevin decided to go along with them. He asked Michele if she wanted to go also. Ordinarily, I would have volunteered to stay with Derek by myself, as I loved to do this, but that morning I was relieved when Michele said she was tired and would stay with me and Derek.

Around noon I told Michele I thought we should take Derek to the hospital. Since we had already called Derek's regular doctor and could not bring him to CPRI, our alternative was the local hospital. When we called first to see who was on call, the doctor on call was one Michele did not like so we decided to go to the Children's Hospital of Western Ontario, a hospital where Derek had never been. I don't know why we thought of that hospital.

As we were leaving the house, Danny touched Derek's head and whispered to me, "He's not coming back, is he?" I couldn't answer that. I could not admit the reality. I still hoped my faith would make God perform a miracle.

I drove us to the hospital. On the way, Michele sat in the back seat holding Derek and his portable oxygen tank. He was restful on the drive so when we arrived at the hospital, we drove around the block, thinking maybe he was better and we could just go home. I knew differently although I don't know why. I knew I didn't want Derek to die at home.

We went in to the ER. The doctor who was there was excellent and I believe God arranged for her to be there just for

Derek. I felt like now that we were in the hospital, Derek would be okay. The doctors and nurses were in charge so I thought they could somehow save him from dying. Derek had been at most other hospitals but not this one. Maybe, oh maybe, it was God's plan that the people at this hospital would perform the miracle.

> *Often we recall clear details of events that lead up to something difficult. If you have lost someone special, do you have significant special memories you like to recall?*
>
> *Have you ever hoped against hope that maybe if you went to a different hospital or did things a different way, maybe God would answer your prayer at last? Has it ever worked out that way?*
>
> *Sometimes it is too hard for us to speak or even admit the reality of something that is happening to us. Has this ever happened to you?*

4

How does one speak words of death when holding a little boy? Michele called Kevin to let him know we were at the hospital, the doctor was good and things were going to be okay. But that was an illusion. *Okay* did not mean that Derek was going to live, and I sensed Michele and Kevin knew that as well. When the nurse put the monitors on Derek, it became apparent his body was shutting down.

I will never forget the moment when I realized what was happening and I said to Michele that Derek was dying. The cry that escaped from Michele's throat is forever etched in my memory. I was sitting on the hospital bed holding Derek as this kept him calm.

It was at that moment I realized that my hope was more about my faith in faith than my faith in God.

But I also realized that no matter what I want, God will have his way. No amount of my positive energy could change that. Just thinking positive thoughts was not helping me.

God doesn't care if I have a master's degree in positive thinking or meditation. He doesn't need me to have dealt with all my doubts and fears (of which, believe me, I have many). In fact the Bible gives many examples of people who had faith and did not get what they wanted, or thought God should give them. In other words their faith did not fix anything although they were doing God's will for their lives.

I have learned that faith in God can lead to healing—and then again it can and will lead to death of a grandson. This is God's will, not mine. God's will is that Derek did not have a long earthly life but he has the gift of eternal life.

My experience with Derek taught me that faith is not a skill that I need to learn, nor is it positive visualization, magic or a miracle where, if I have enough faith, things will happen as I want.

My faith is based on biblical principles that say that when I follow God I will always end up where I need to be. It doesn't matter if others think all is lost. I am where I should be. And so is Derek.

Is your faith in faith or in God? What is the difference?

What role does positive thinking and visualization play in your understanding of healing?

How can we be where we need to be if everything looks like all is lost?

5

Michele went back to the phone to call Kevin with the truth. I can only imagine that heartbreaking conversation.

Jason drove Kevin to the hospital; Jason stayed for a while and then left. I told Kevin and Michele that if they wanted we could take Derek back home, but they agreed it was best to stay at the hospital.

Michele called her friend Wendy who had been at Derek's birth and who came to join us at the hospital. Michele's mother, father and sister also came. Everyone took turns holding Derek. I did not want to let him go.

Wendy held the oxygen to his mouth as the mask on his face was irritating him. All other monitors were removed.

All night he gasped for breath as his lungs filled up with fluid. All night I kept repeating, "Please, Lord, have mercy." My precious little Derek heaving, gasping with that dreadful sound of laboured breathing.

How long would he last? How long could his little heart keep beating? Should I ask God to bring Derek back or to release him from his pain? I didn't know. I just prayed for God to have mercy.

It felt surreal to hold Derek and stroke his head. I couldn't say the word *goodbye* to Derek but I was doing goodbye.

Michele took Derek in her arms and then he was gone. It is impossible to describe my feelings. I could only gasp in agony. I will forever remember the doctor's word, as she looked at Kevin: "His heart has *stopped.*" That was all she said.

That strong little heart had stopped beating. As I held Derek that night, the little boy I loved was disappearing before my eyes. I couldn't look at the lightness of him as his life energy started to leave.

How do you pray when you don't know what to pray for? What does praying for mercy do in these circumstances?

How can family come together around someone as they are dying?

Have you ever been with someone as they died or after they died? Was the experience what you thought it would be? Is it painful to remember or do you remember it as a blessing?

6

Everywhere I look, I see books and advertising that tell me that living a simple life will bring me less stress and more contentment and happiness.

Derek lived a simple life. He wanted to be fed, kept clean, and warm. Oh, how he loved his bath and to swim in a warm pool. He wanted to be held continually and loved. Derek participated fully in life—he didn't hold anything back.

Derek helped me to start asking different questions of life. To ask what is right with a person before I start to look at what is wrong. This has changed my attitude towards people, things and choices.

Think about this: when you start to look at something first from the negative side, you rarely turn it around to look at the positive. Wouldn't you want to be part of a family that first noticed what was right not wrong with you?

As a Christian, I believe God created me and he created Derek. When I first saw Derek I believed God had a purpose for him and it was good. I remember vividly the first time I saw Derek shortly after his birth. I was told there was something "seriously wrong"—that wrong word again—with him. But, when I looked at him he was the most perfect baby I had ever seen. He was so peaceful. There was such an innocence about him, not the vulnerable, newborn innocence, but a dependable sturdy innocence. He seemed like a little old man in his baby body.

Derek taught me unconditional love. Caring for and loving Derek wasn't about me; it was about him. Derek was never able to care for himself; he was totally cared for by others. Thus the question of what would happen to me if I loved him changed to what would happen to him if I loved him? These questions are the basis of my faith.

The depth of pain I felt over the death of my little Derek is a direct reflection of the love I allowed into my life from him. In other words, if I hadn't loved Derek so much, I would not feel so much.

How would you feel if people first noticed what was right not wrong with you? Do you take that approach to others? How do you think you could move toward that perspective?

What does Derek's story teach you about people's purpose in life? What role does unconditionally loving others play in our life purpose?

If you are experiencing the pain of losing someone you love, how does it feel to realize that you wouldn't feel so much if you hadn't loved so much?

Derek with his Grandpa G beside the Christmas tree

Derek, Lindsay and me

7

Michele asked me if I would speak at Derek's funeral, but the task seemed too large for me. In my own strength I could not do it. But for Derek, anything was possible including things I thought were impossible. I have always used words to frame my experiences, but how could I speak about Derek, a little boy who spoke not a word verbally?

These are the words I spoke at Derek's funeral service:

Words are so inadequate to describe our little Derek. In fact I had a hard time finding them. Derek, our little angel, spoke to us without words. Everywhere we look today there are reminders of him, his pictures at home, his bed, his chairs, his pony and his toys.

Derek was a little boy of extremes. When he was well, his little face would shine with pure joy, especially when his daddy and grandpa would tickle him. Derek loved to play. When he was ill his little spirit fought so hard.

Our family is more compassionate, accepting, kind and loving towards each other for having Derek these past almost seven years. He brought out the best in each of us. His big sister Lindsay who loved and accepted him for the special little person he is. His mom, Michele, who fought like a lion to always get the best for him, whose love was never-ending, His dad, Kevin who never lost patience. Derek is an extension of all the goodness in Kevin. I have never seen a more loving father and son. His grandma Carole and grandpa Frank prayed endlessly for Derek. Grandpa G who loves Derek beyond words. His heart weeps for the little boy we know will always be with us. To me Derek was my little angel who now resides with God in all his perfection. Derek is walking, talking and singing. We are so blessed to have had you, Derek.

(My body was filled with emotion as I struggled to read these words, but as I came to this section, a peace that is beyond anything I have ever felt came over me. I could envision Derek doing all the things little boys would do, such as walk, talk and sing, especially sing in a loud clear voice just like his sister Lindsay.)

Derek has many aunts, uncles, cousins who all have such joy in their hearts as they remember the little sweetheart whose face would light up and who would laugh from his little belly. The many friends, dear Wendy, the doctors, nurses, teachers, neighbours, all who know Derek remember the little boy who fought so hard.

Derek, we cannot hear your laughter or see your smile. How I wish I could rock you a little while. I know you are seeing everything we do. You taught us that life is much too short and precious, that at any time could end. You taught us that a family and love is more special than diamonds or money. At the end of one's life on earth it will not matter if you missed a day of school or work. No one will care about what brand of clothes you wore. What will be remembered is the joy and love you share.

While our hearts grieve over your loss, we rejoice that your spirit is in peace. As Jesus said: let the little children come to me and do not forbid them, for of such is the kingdom of heaven. Amen.

As you think about the eulogy given at the end of Derek's short life, spend time thinking about what you would like said at your funeral.

What would you hope people would remember about you and the way you lived? How might that change how you live today?

After the death of a loved one who has struggled with illness, have you ever had an experience of rejoicing that they are now healed and well? If not, spend a few minutes in prayer asking God to show you this healing.

Derek and Lindsay

8

"Here is your little angel," the sales clerk said as she handed me my nicely wrapped garden figurine. She had no idea that I had purchased this to help motivate me to write about my real angel, Derek. Little did I myself realize that it was not motivation I needed but courage, the courage to take the first step—or in this case to write the first word.

Since his birth, I had called Derek my little angel, but I wondered what an angel looked like. According to Larry Libby in his book, *Somewhere Angels*, when angels appear to people on earth, they have a beauty that almost makes you afraid. That was Derek.

As I look at this figurine of a little boy with curly hair, wings on his back, hands folded, a peaceful look on his face sitting on top of a round globe, it does remind me of my little Derek. I reach over to touch the figure's head and remember the soft curly hair of my beloved grandson, and I ache to look into the deep blue of Derek's eyes.

In the Bible there are times when angels looked just like people. In Genesis 18:2-5, the three men who came to visit Jesus were not men but God and two angels in the likeness of humans.

Was Derek a "real" angel? I will not know until I get to heaven. But heaven has become a real place to me now that Derek is there.

The Bible does not tell us a lot about heaven, possibly because it is difficult to get our mortal minds to understand it. I don't know the answer. However the Bible does tell us that heaven is a real place, with real people living there. Revelation 21: 4, 5 says,

He will wipe away every tear from their eyes. Death will be no more. There will be no mourning, crying or pain anymore, for the former things have passed away. Then the one seated on the throne said, "Look! I am making all things new!" He also said, "Write this down, for these words are trustworthy and true."

I cling to these words of faith. There will be no broken bodies, no feeding tubes, no oxygen masks, no hospitals, no good-byes, no funerals.

I now no longer believe in God. I now *know* God. God himself has changed Derek. This happened instantaneously, "in the twinkling of an eye" Derek was dressed for heaven. The Bible tells us in 1 Corinthians 15:51-53*:*

Listen, I'm telling you a secret: all of us won't die, but we will all be changed— in an instant, in the blink of an eye, at the final trumpet. The trumpet will blast, and the dead will be raised with bodies that won't decay, and we will be changed. It's necessary for this rotting body to be clothed with what can't decay, and for the body that is dying to be clothed in what can't die.

I am certain that Jesus overcame death and arose from the dead. This is a historical fact not my feelings. Thus, although I sorrow because Derek is no longer physically with us, I can rejoice that he is in heaven.

*Have you ever met someone and wondered if they might be an angel? Hebrews 13:2 tells us, "*Don't neglect to open up your homes to guests, because by doing this some have been hosts to angels without knowing it.*" How does this idea change how you might treat people?*

What makes heaven real to you? Do you ever struggle with the idea of heaven?

What can you rejoice in after the death of someone you love? What is the source of that assurance?

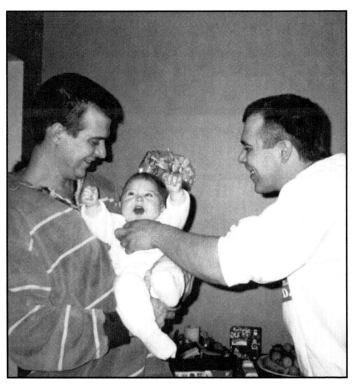

*Derek held by his dad, Kevin,
while being tickled by his Uncle Kenny*

9

THERE ARE SO MANY THINGS ABOUT LIFE THAT I DO NOT KNOW and cannot explain. Derek's birth and death raised questions I cannot even begin to answer.

Why did this happen to Derek, and my son and my family?

Where was my hope as I watched Derek's wee body deteriorate further and further?

Why did Derek's suffering make us more tender and loving to each other rather than bitter?

Where do I and my family go from here now that Derek is no longer the thread that seemed to hold us all together?

In his absence will small things drive us apart?

Will my faith survive Derek's death?

I believed God would answer my prayers to completely heal Derek's disability—did this not happen because I did not believe enough? Why did God not heal Derek?

During Derek's short life I had hope that he would be healed. Sure, technology kept him alive but faith, love and commitment from the people who loved him was what gave Derek a life. After his death, I struggled (and struggle) with the "no" answers.

Then one day I came across this poem:

> *God answers prayers, sometimes, when hearts are weak,*
> *He gives the very gifts believers seek.*
> *But often faith must learn a deeper rest,*
> *And trust God's silence when He does not speak;*
> *For He whose name is Love will send the best.*
> *Stars may burn out, nor mountain walls endure,*
> *But God is true, His promises are sure.*
> *He is our strength.*
> (M. G. Plantz)

Some people believe that when tragedy comes to them they have done wrong and God is punishing them. In fact, I have family members who say that if you have a disabled child you are being punished for an unforgivable sin.

Others told me the pain of losing a child can either spiritually make or break you; it can either kill one's soul or bring it to life.

For me the loss of Derek caused my aching soul to draw closer to my faith in God. Without that faith, Derek's struggle was meaningless.

I looked for wisdom in human stories and readings but their truth always fall short. Instead, when I struggle with these questions and interpretations, I turn to God's word, the Bible. 1 Corinthians 2: 9-12 tells me:

> *But this is precisely what is written: God has prepared things for those who love him that no eye has seen, or ear has heard, or that haven't crossed the mind of any human being. God has revealed these things to us through the Spirit. The Spirit searches everything, including the depths of God. Who knows a person's depths except their own spirit that lives in them? In the same way, no one has known the depths of God except God's Spirit. We haven't received the world's spirit but God's Spirit so that we can know the things given to us by God.*

God doesn't send us our problems but He does allow us to go through them. God's purpose is in changing me, not the circumstance. Thus even though not all my questions were answered the way I hoped they would be, my faith tells me Derek's disability was not a punishment but a blessing.

Can I not leave the unanswerable questions of Derek's life and death with the God who created him? All of my questions will have answers one day.

> *What questions have you asked when faced with tragedy or times of deep sorrow? Does voicing those questions help even if they cannot be answered?*

What do you do when you feel your prayers are unanswered or God says no? What biblical truths do you rest upon?

When you have struggled, did you draw near to God or did God feel far away? What does the Bible teach us about God's presence in times of human sorrow? See Psalm 34:18.

Derek at his birth with sister Lindsay

10

As I flew back to British Columbia to continue my work, a voice in my head said, "What will people say? You should have stayed with your family." But this voice was that of a woman who was concerned about what others would think, who was afraid.

Fear has always been in the fabric of my life, but since that night when I held Derek as he was dying, I was no longer afraid in the same way. Since Derek's birth I had always been afraid he would die. That night was different. I was peaceful, praying only that God would have mercy and take his spirit quickly from his physical body.

Fear has not completely disappeared, but I am no longer afraid of living, doing, taking risks. *Just do it* has always been my motto. Derek has taught me there is something more painful than the death that took his little body from this world—a life lived in fear leaves too many moments and opportunities unlived.

Derek's life has taught me that for the second part of my life I want to do only that which really matters. I refused to go back to being that other woman who was afraid of what others thought.

What role has fear played in your life? What does it say to you?

How would you live differently if you weren't afraid?

Derek and Lindsay and me hanging out after Christmas morning

11

As I returned to Revelstoke, everything everywhere spoke of Derek.

As I walked into my office at the hospital in Revelstoke, I saw a couple, both sitting in wheelchairs. I stopped, made eye contact, and we talked about the weather. I did not know this man and woman but somehow in his blue eyes I saw Derek who had the same wise blue eyes. I had heard bits and pieces of information about this man from co-workers. Apparently he had worked as a teacher then a counselor in the school system. He was in the hospital because he had cancer and was "really sick". This made me think of how we often referred to Derek as being "really sick".

Soon after this, I was drawn to attend an art exhibit. I found myself standing in front of an abstract painting of water and mountains that resembled Derek. As the tears came to my eyes I knew I needed this painting. I purchased it.

I saw Derek in the water, the mountains, the sunshine, little children. I didn't want Derek in heaven. I wanted him here with his family.

And I struggled as I returned to my mental health therapist job in Revelstoke. Everything seemed so unimportant. I also could not continue to listen to the sorrows of others, sorrows much like mine. I took some time away from my work.

I could not cry, nothing seemed right and there was nothing I could fix. What others said to me in an effort to help only increased my pain. Comments spoke with good intentions—he is in heaven now, he doesn't have to suffer—did not help me. All I could think was *how would you like your grandchild to die at age seven?*

Night and day I prayed, even when it seemed I could not pray. I believe God heard my cries, because now I can write these words. Derek's life is not lost.

Where have you tried to find comfort after the death of someone you love? What has actually been comforting? How does this idea change how you might treat people?

How have others tried to comfort you? What was actually comforting?

Do you believe that tears can be a form of prayer? What does Romans 8:26 teach us about how God hears our cries and groans and responds to us when we are beyond words?

12

DEATH, OF COURSE, MAKES EVERYTHING MORE CLEAR.

The "should haves" and "what ifs" were a big part of my questions when Derek died. However, I knew that it wasn't wise or healthy to dwell on my regrets. This self-inflicted punishment would not change the decisions I made, nor would they bring Derek back to life.

As I looked ahead after Derek's death, though, I did all the things they tell you in therapy not to do—in December 2005, I left a job I loved, and moved across Canada back to Ontario.

Despite the fact that I saw Derek everywhere—in the blue eyes of a dying man, in the blue of an artist's painting, in the clear blue of the mountain waters—I needed to be in Derek's place, his house, his room.

For a time, I slept in his room with all of his most special things— his baseball cap, his shoes, the butterflies hanging from the ceiling that I bought him for his fourth birthday.

It felt right and peaceful. Just like my times spent rocking Derek.

I took out the little white horse I had bought for him and which was one of his favourite things. I wanted to smell his smell but it was gone.

Some say you get over the grief of death with time, while others say you live around it. My experience is that you daily live it. I would drive Lindsay to school, the same school that Derek attended, I was so grateful to be able to do this. Sometimes I would watch a video of Derek with Michele. My heart ached for both of us as the tears streamed down our faces, neither one of us making a sound.

I have learned that there is no such thing as closure or that I can somehow recover from Derek's death—as if there ever will be a time when I will no longer miss my little boy. I believe there is no timeline to grief and I really dislike lumping my grief into stages. Sometimes without rhyme or reason my yearning to hold Derek and the loss of him is so unbearable.

What clarity has death brought to you? Are there changes you have made after someone you love has died? Are there changes you should make?

Have you ever done something small or big that you might think was silly but that brought you great comfort?

Do you believe we ever fully recover from grief? What are your expectations for this?

13

For someone who was not able to speak words—Derek communicated volumes. His eyes held more love than most people might ever imagine possible. He had the spirit of a fighter. He lived life to the fullest of his abilities. He lived in the moment, in tune with people and his surroundings.

Caring for Derek and his needs brought me back to the basics of life. Derek's beautiful body showed us hope, determination and life itself.

When I was with Derek time slowed down. No, let me reword that—I slowed down. Rocking him in silence the peace I felt went far beyond any words. Derek was my forever baby who would curl his little body and later his bigger body to fit mine and sleep contently for hours.

I never made excuses for Derek's behaviour. I didn't explain why he drooled and made noises. Nor why he couldn't pick up his head.

When I looked at him he was the most beautiful little boy I've ever seen. I am not talking about the beauty you can see with your eyes but the beauty I felt in my heart.

Derek did not like to be alone; he wanted to feel the presence of another. Derek loved to be at home, home for Derek was where his loved ones were, his family and those who cared for him. I have realized through Derek that home is the rightness I feel whenever I am where I know I am loved.

Like me, Derek wanted people to pay attention to him. However, out in public, Derek easily became invisible. Many people treated him like he was not able to communicate; they did not talk or touch him. Although others didn't really come out and say it, they were afraid of him. It is tragic so few got to really know him.

His spirit gave me the strength and faith to keep fighting for him—and now, for myself. I have faith that I am doing the right thing and that it could make a difference.

Francis of Assisi once said, "Preach the gospel; use words if necessary." How did a wordless boy communicate so clearly? How and what do we communicate without words?

Who is the most beautiful person you know? What makes them truly beautiful?

Who are the people who might easily be invisible to you? How might you let go of your fear in order to see and hear them? How might you be changed by this?

14

A decade has now passed since Derek went to heaven. For years after Derek died, I had recurring bad dreams about babies and children dying—or being unable to die. My fears would assault me. What if God's promises are not true? What if there is no life after death.

I turned to my Bible for truth. 1 Thessalonians 4:13-18 says:

Brothers and sisters, we want you to know about people who have died so that you won't mourn like others who don't have any hope. Since we believe that Jesus died and rose, so we also believe that God will bring with him those who have died in Jesus. What we are saying is a message from the Lord: we who are alive and still around at the Lord's coming definitely won't go ahead of those who have died. This is because the Lord himself will come down from heaven with the signal of a shout by the head angel and a blast on God's trumpet. First, those who are dead in Christ will rise. Then, we who are living and still around will be taken up together with them in the clouds to meet with the Lord in the air. That way we will always be with the Lord. So encourage each other with these words.

My faith and energy are renewed. I struggle not to question Derek's death but simply accept it. It may sound simple but is not easy.

I know it is time to get my writings published. Why did I not do this sooner? Why wait ten years? I know the answer, which is simple, really. Because, the words are so very personal, I did not think they were good enough to be published, or that anyone would care to read them. However, I've realized it is important to me that Derek's legacy is published not only in the hearts of his loved ones but on paper as well.

I need to tell you a bit about how Derek's legacy has shaped where I am today. Once again I am living in Ontario. I left a job in Alberta. (I will write about why and how in my next book.)

Watching Derek I learned that life is short and that I need to figure out what is important to keep and what to get rid of. Many things in my life are not always clear to me but I know that when my heart and soul are not in what I am doing or where I am living, it is time to change. I have also learned that even when I make changes, sometimes I find myself in a place where I am not meant to stay. As I continue to find my place in this world, I have learned that what I wanted in my forties or fifties is not what I need in my sixties.

Because of Derek I have learned that home is not a place, but the rightness I feel whenever I know I am loved, or where I have someone I can love. Sometimes that is family; most times it is not. Just as Derek struggled to breathe in and out, my own life builds up, changes and then changes again.

I have also learned that I need to accept staying so that I can go. Derek's legacy is the lesson that life is precious—both strong and fragile at the same time. He left me the legacy of hope which cannot be found by looking back but by moving forward.

Let me leave you with a final precious Scripture verse: "*God so loved the world that he gave his only Son, so that everyone who believes in him won't perish but will have eternal life*" (John 3: 16).